AF266626

The **Minor Prophets**

Who Are They?

Beverly A. Scanlon

WESTBOW
PRESS®
A DIVISION OF THOMAS NELSON
& ZONDERVAN

WestBow Press books may be ordered through booksellers or by contacting:

WestBow Press
A Division of Thomas Nelson & Zondervan
1663 Liberty Drive
Bloomington, IN 47403
www.westbowpress.com
1 (866) 928-1240

ISBN: 978-1-9736-0827-1 (sc)
ISBN: 978-1-9736-0828-8 (e)

Library of Congress Control Number: 2017917988

Print information available on the last page.

WestBow Press rev. date: 1/17/2018

In memory of my daughter,
Kendra Lyn Waters Keeney,
1966–1998:
my inspiration to experience life fully.

Contents

Here's the Buzz.

📖 There are thirty-nine books in the Old Testament.
📖 There are twenty-seven books in the New Testament.
📖 There are twelve minor prophets.
📖 They are minor prophets because their books are shorter.

- The book of Jonah is the thirty-second book in the Old Testament.
- Jonah was the fifth of the twelve minor prophets.
- *Jonah* means *dove*.

- The book of Nahum is the thirty-fourth book in the Old Testament.
- Nahum was the seventh of the twelve minor prophets.
- *Nahum* means *comfort* or *comforter*.

- The book of Obadiah is the thirty-first book in the Old Testament.
- Obadiah is the fourth of the twelve minor prophets.
- *Obadiah* means *servant of Yahweh*.
- There are at least eight people named Obadiah in the Old Testament.

Messages of the Prophets

Prophet	Workplace	Estimated Year of Message	Heart of the Message
Hosea	Israel	750–722 BC	faithfulness
Joel	Judah	835–796 BC	repentance
Amos	Judah	760–750 BC	blessings
Obadiah	Edom	585–550 BC	restoration
Jonah	Nineveh, Assyria	750 BC	compassion
Micah	Judah	700 BC	justice
Nahum	Nineveh, Assyria	650 BC	comfort
Habakkuk	Judah	610 BC	integrity
Zephaniah	Judah	625 BC	humility, mercy
Haggai	Judah	520 BC	priorities
Zechariah	Judah	518 BC	hope
Malachi	Judah	450 BC or 420 BC	worship

The Story of Jonah

Minor Prophet #5: Jonah, the Rebellious One

"Jonah swallowed by a whale!" This could have been the headline for the book of Jonah. But the real story is about how Jonah ran from God and about God's forgiving heart.

Jonah's story begins when God asked him to go to Nineveh, Assyria. This was about 750 BC. *BC* signifies the number of years before Jesus Christ was born. The people of Nineveh were brutal warriors, worshipped false idols, stampeded other countries, stole, and were just plain evil and wicked. God wanted Jonah to warn them that their city would be destroyed if they did not change their evil ways.

At the time, Jonah was in the seaport of Joppa. Nineveh was not that far away.

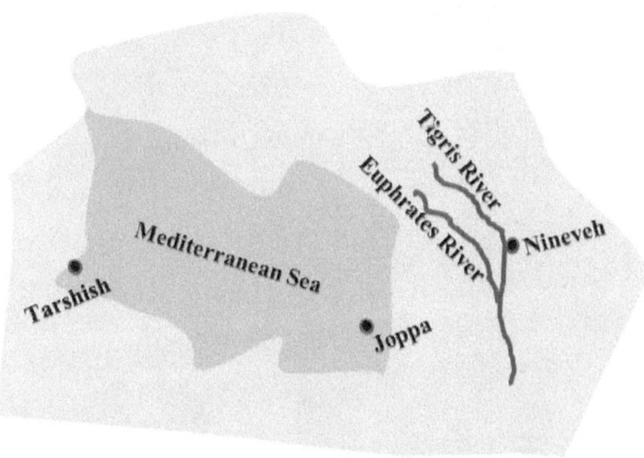

But Jonah didn't care about the distance. He felt that it was a waste of time to warn them. He did not want to go! Have you ever been asked to do something you did not want to do?

Jonah put his thinking cap on and came up with a plan.

"Aha!" he thought. "I will go the other way, to Tarshish, and escape from God!"

Just then there was a ship sailing across the Mediterranean Sea to Tarshish. How lucky was that? Jonah got on that ship.

"Whew," he thought, "that was close. But I got away. God can't possibly ask me to go to Nineveh now."

While on the way to Tarshish, the seas became very choppy. The fishermen on the ship knew that Jonah was a man of God. They, however, worshipped other gods. They thought that if they prayed to their gods, the seas would calm down. Unfortunately, none of the fishermen's prayers to their gods calmed the seas.

Because their prayers to their gods did not work, they thought the stormy seas must be caused by Jonah's God. So the sailors went down to the lower level of the ship where Jonah was taking a nap. Can you believe it? He was sleeping while the ship rocked violently back and forth!

The sailors yelled at Jonah, "Get up! We could all die in this storm. The seas were calm until you came aboard! Your God must be unhappy with you. What must you do to make him happy again?"

Jonah heard what they were saying. He hung his head and told them that he knew why the seas were so rough.

Jonah said, "God will calm the seas if you throw me overboard. It is my fault because I disobeyed God. I was to go to Nineveh but ran the other way instead." So they threw Jonah into the raging waters. The seas became calm again.

The fishermen saw the power of Jonah's God. They offered the Lord a sacrifice and made vows to worship him.

Now Jonah was in the giant sea, all alone, and he felt panic. What would happen to him now? He felt so alone. He began to pray and asked God to forgive him for disobeying. Just then, a huge fish (not a whale) came along and swallowed him.

"Oh, no!" Jonah yelled out loud. "What do I do now?"

Can you name a time when you felt scared, but God took care of you?

It sounds very icky to be in the dark, smelly, slimy belly of a big fish. It does not sound like a place where one would choose to pray. But Jonah was grateful to be alive, so he continued to pray to God: "Please, God, keep me safe. I am sorry that I disobeyed you." Jonah prayed to God constantly.

God kept him in the fish's belly a total of three days and three nights. (Ever wonder why it was so long?) Finally, at God's command, the big fish spat Jonah out onto the shore. He was all bleached out, bald, and smelly. But he didn't care.

He was thankful that God had kept him safe. He was now ready to go to Nineveh and deliver God's message. Perhaps it would have been easier to go there in the first place. What do you think?

So Jonah started out for Nineveh. He discovered that it was a very large city. The Ninevites had built walls a hundred feet thick around the city and a sixty-foot moat (a deep ditch filled with water) to keep all their treasures safe and other warriors out of their territory. The city was so large that it took Jonah three days (there's that *three* again) to walk through the entire city.

As he walked, Jonah told the people of the coming doom. God was going to destroy their city because of their horrible wickedness. The king of Nineveh heard the message and believed Jonah. He told the people of Nineveh, "We must give up our evil ways so that we are not destroyed!"

When the people of Nineveh heard God's message from the king, they repented immediately. God was pleased that they repented, and he did not destroy the city. The people of Nineveh cheered mightily.

"Praise God," they shouted!

After Jonah delivered the message from God, he stomped to the mountain's top. He was angry that God had spared the city of Nineveh because the people had repented. But God took care of Jonah again. He sprouted a large plant that protected Jonah from the hot sun. Jonah just sat there and fumed.

Have you ever been angry because someone didn't get the punishment you thought that person deserved?

Before long, God got tired of Jonah's pouting. He sent a

strong, hot wind that wilted the plant. Then a worm crawled up the plant and ate the remaining leaves. The wind and the storm totally destroyed the plant, and Jonah was left in the hot sun.

Now Jonah was really, really angry!

God asked Jonah, "Why are you so angry? I saved you. Why should I not save the people of Nineveh?"

Jonah just sat there and pouted. Then he said, "This is so unfair! I spent three days in a dark, smelly fish's belly, walked for miles and miles, and now I have sunburn because my shade is gone! I don't get it!"

But God is patient. He waited for Jonah to think about all the events. Slowly the actions of God made sense to Jonah. God had protected him in the fish's belly even though he had disobeyed God. God had provided a plant for cover even though Jonah was planning to cheer when Nineveh was destroyed. And then God had gotten Jonah's attention by destroying his shade with a hot wind and a worm.

God knows we forget him sometimes and do things that are sinful and not pleasing to God. But God is patient. He loves us and will forgive us when we ask.

God's lesson was about listening to him and his compassionate heart. Even if we try to ignore him, he is there waiting for us. After all Jonah's trials, he understood at last. Do you?

Why did God put Jonah in the belly of a big fish?

Why did God decide to spare Nineveh?

Has there been a time when you did not want to forgive someone?

Jonah 3:10

When God saw their deeds, that they turned from their wicked way, then God relented concerning the calamity which he had declared he would bring upon them. And he did not do it.

James 1:2–5

Consider it pure joy, my brothers and sisters whenever you face trials of many kinds, because you know that the testing of your faith produces perseverance. Let perseverance finish its work so that you may be mature and complete, not lacking anything. If any of you lacks wisdom, you should ask God, who gives generously to all without finding fault, and it will be given to you.

Prayer

Dear heavenly Father, help me remember the story of Jonah and the message in the story. I realize that if I do bad things, I need to ask your forgiveness. I also know that I need to listen to you. Help me be patient for your answers to my prayers. Protect me as you did Jonah when I am stubborn and help me see the way that you want me to go. In your name I pray. Amen.

Puzzle

The Story of Nahum

Prophet #7: Nahum, the Bearer of Bad News

Nahum was a prophet from approximately 650 to 625 BC. Remember—BC means the number of years before Jesus Christ was born. Nahum served about a hundred years after Jonah. He was a special messenger sent by God to Nineveh, Assyria. Nahum was to deliver the *same* message that Jonah had given to the Ninevites. Hmm … why did Nahum have to do the same thing Jonah had already done?

Well, Jonah had been sent to tell the Ninevites to stop their killing, stampeding, stealing, and worship of false idols and urge them to give up their totally wicked ways. That is quite a list! When Jonah got to Nineveh, the king of Nineveh heard his message and believed him. The king of Nineveh knew the message was from God and believed that God would destroy the city if the Ninevites did not change their evil ways. So the king of Nineveh ordered everyone to call on God. The people of Nineveh had repented of their sins, and God spared their city.

If God had spared their city a hundred years ago, why would he not spare it again?

Have you ever been told several times to stop doing something? Sometimes, when we are asked to stop doing a wrong thing too many times, we may start to ignore the request. Or if we continue to do the wrong thing without ever getting punished, why would we start doing the right thing? It is easy to say that we will stop doing the wrong thing. It is also easy to forget that there will be consequences if we continue to do the wrong thing.

Have you ever broken a rule?

These two children are breaking a rule. The rule isn't a major one, but signs in plain sight are telling them not to do something! And they are doing it anyway!

Well, to say the Ninevites were "breaking the rules" is a major understatement. After Jonah delivered the message and they repented, the Ninevites gradually went back to all their wicked and evil ways. They once again started worshiping false idols and stealing valuables and killing people in other cities. They regained their title as the mightiest city on earth, and they once again thought and believed they were invincible. You can almost hear them pounding on their chests in their pride.

But when the Assyrians attacked and killed his people in Israel, God had had enough. He was going to destroy their powerful city, Nineveh. And to top it off, the king of Assyria had forced the king of Judah to pay far more taxes than necessary. The lands of Israel and Judah were God's promised lands for his people. God was furious about the way the Assyrians had treated his people and destroyed the lands of Israel and Judah.

But God is compassionate. He gives people plenty of opportunities to do what is right. He wanted to give Nineveh another chance, so he sent Nahum to Nineveh to warn them again and give them one last chance to stop their wickedness.

This time the Ninevites did not repent. After all, theirs was the mightiest city in the world, and they believed nothing bad could ever happen to them. They even had food stored up to feed 120,000 people for twenty years! Think how much food that would be!

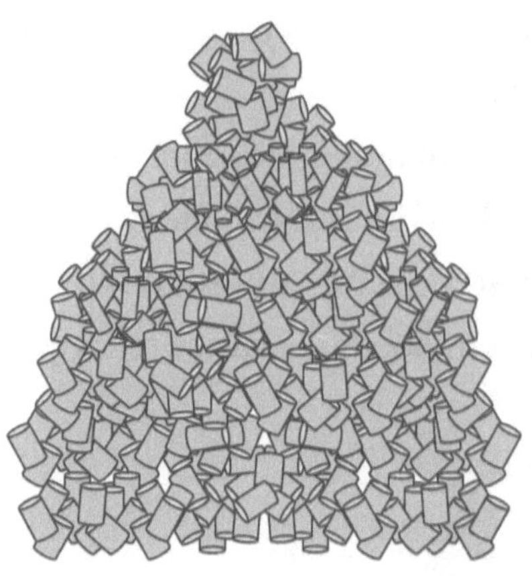

Think about food storage. How much food does your family have stored up for emergencies?

Nahum gathered the people of Nineveh to give God's warning. He told them about Thebes, the capital of Egypt that had been destroyed by God in 656 BC because of the people's evil and wicked actions.

"What in the world does that have to do with us?" they shouted. The Ninevites did not see how what happened to Thebes had anything to do with them. They did not realize they had performed the same evil and wicked actions that the Thebans had. It is really sad when people don't realize they are doing bad things. The people of Nineveh were like that. They thought and believed they could do anything they wanted since they lived in the mightiest city in the world! (Hear that pounding on their chests again?)

So Nahum delivered the bad news: Either stop the wickedness, killing, stealing, torturing, and worship of false idols or your city will be destroyed!

They didn't listen. For ten years, nothing happened. Perhaps God was giving the Ninevites one last chance to repent and change their evil and wicked ways. But the Ninevites still didn't believe that anything bad would happen to them. (Hear that pounding on the chests one last time?)

But God does not forget. In 612 BC, a huge flood from the Tigris River broke open the gates of the hundred-foot walls of Nineveh. The Babylonians and Medes marched into the city, cheering, and destroyed everything. Nineveh was taken to the ground. Ninevites were captured, taken to other countries, or killed. All the valuables of the mighty Assyrians were stolen. To this day, Nineveh is a massive mound of sand and has never been rebuilt.

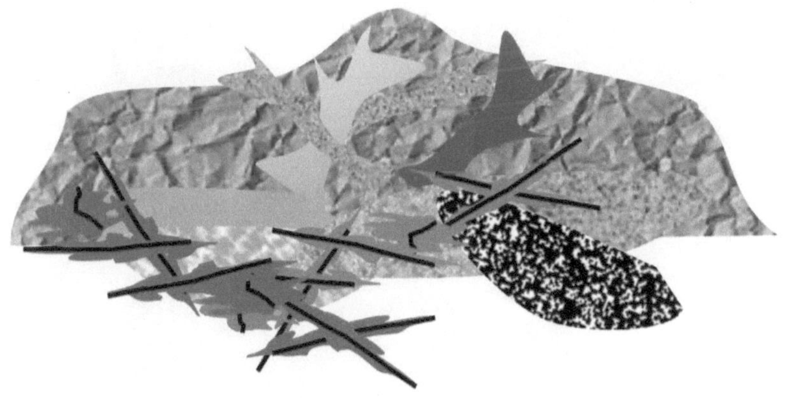

Let's review. Nahum's name means *comfort*. One might wonder how comfort can be found in this story. Comfort comes to those who believe in God and trust him. God comforted and protected his lands and people in Israel and Judah when the wicked and evil actions of the Assyrians did not stop. He had given the rule-breakers plenty of chances to repent, but they chose not to listen. Comfort came to the believers from Israel and Judah when the Assyrians were punished. They rejoiced that the city of Nineveh was destroyed and the Assyrians were defeated. It comforted the Israelites that God was protecting them from the brutal acts that they had experienced.

How do you feel when someone who has done wrong is punished?

How do you feel when someone who has done wrong is NOT punished?

How do we find comfort in the story of Nahum?

Nahum 1:7

The Lord is good, a refuge in times of trouble. He cares for those who trust in Him.

James 1:2–5

[2] Consider it pure joy, my brothers and sisters whenever you face trials of many kinds,[3] because you know that the testing of your faith produces perseverance.[4] Let perseverance finish its work so that you may be mature and complete, not lacking anything.[5] If any of you lacks wisdom, you should ask God, who gives generously to all without finding fault, and it will be given to you.

Prayer

Dear heavenly Father, help me remember Nahum's message that you are a safe place when I ask for forgiveness. I know that you will bring comfort to me when I ask and obey. I pray for guidance and wisdom so that I may help others to know your love and the comfort of your word. Help me remember you are always with me. In your name I pray. Amen.

Unscramble the words.

hmnau	
btseeh	
nvenihe	
tcmroof	
urstt	
ufrege	
amot	

The Story of Obadiah

Prophet #4: Obadiah, the Man with a Vision

The book of Obadiah is the shortest book in the Old Testament of the Bible. It has only one chapter! The meaning of Obadiah's name gives us a clue to Obadiah's message and mission. His name means *servant of Yahweh. Yahweh* is another Hebrew name for God. Obadiah had a vision from God/Yahweh to go to Edom and warn the Edomites of their coming destruction. Wanting to be obedient and please God, Obadiah set off to complete this dangerous and uncomfortable mission. The Edomites were brutal warriors who fought against the Israelites. The Edomites killed and kidnapped the Israelites, stole their valuables, and were generally wicked people. Obadiah's mission was to tell the Edomites that because of their evil and wicked ways, God was going to destroy their city.

Wait a minute! Jonah and Nahum, also minor prophets, had delivered exactly the same message to Nineveh years before. Nineveh had been the most powerful city in the world at the time of its destruction in 612 BC. The Assyrians had mistreated God's people, destroyed valuables, and killed people in other cities.

Like the Ninevites, the Edomites thought they were safe and secure from God's wrath partly because of where they lived. Edom was situated on the other side of the Dead Sea, across from Judah. The Dead Sea has one entrance and no exit. The Dead Sea has so much salt and such large amounts of minerals that nothing can live in it! In fact, at one time it was called the Salt Sea. The steep hills around the Dead Sea are primarily limestone, and there are hundreds of caves in the hills. These caves provided perfect spots for bandits, like the Edomites, to store their stolen goods, hide from enemies, and easily attack anyone unfamiliar with the maze of caves. Because the caves practically guaranteed their safety, the Edomites had absolutely no fear of being attacked by enemy armies, and they certainly had no fear of God.

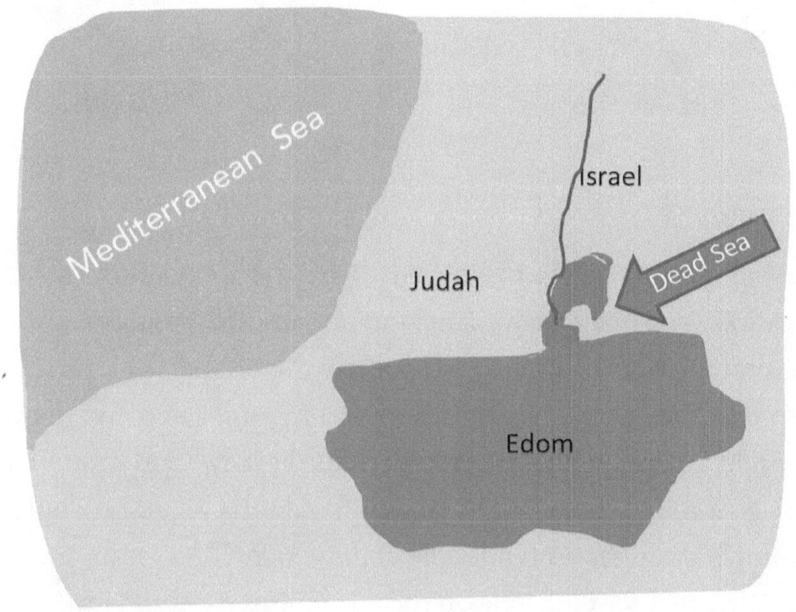

To understand the importance of Obadiah's vision and mission from God, we need to understand the deep history of Edom itself. The foundation of Edom's history is like a puzzle. Once we put each piece together, it will make perfect sense.

Abraham was chosen by God to be the foundation of his nation. God made a covenant—an unbreakable promise—with Abraham. God promised to multiply Abraham's descendants so that they would be as numerous as the stars, and Abraham would be the father of many nations. Finally, God promised to give the entire land of Canaan to Abraham's descendants. Simple promises with a simple ending, right? Not at all!

In order for God to keep these promises to Abraham, God was going to have to perform a few miracles. First, although Abraham was married, he and his wife Sarah had no children. This was a big deal since Sarah was around sixty-five years old at the time, and Abraham was seventy-five years old at the time God made his covenant with Abraham! Abraham could not understand how he and Sarah, who were already too old to have children, were going to have even one baby—let alone thousands of descendants! Besides, Abraham and Sarah were on their way to Egypt at the time God made this promise. But God is not limited by time or place. God is the God of miracles! When Abraham was a hundred years old and Sarah was ninety years old, Sarah miraculously had a baby boy. Abraham and Sarah named their baby boy Isaac.

Puzzle #2: Isaac and Rebekah

When Isaac grew up, he married Rebekah. Rebekah became pregnant with twins. We can read that story in Genesis 25:21. Even while Rebekah carried them, the boys were at war with each other. Rebekah cried out, "Why is this happening to me?" In answer to her anguished cry, God told Rebekah that her sons would become two powerful nations one day. These nations would continually be at war with each other, and the older son would serve the younger son.

Through the story, we see that all God's words to Rebekah came true! Remember—God keeps all his promises. Do you keep the promises you make?

Puzzle #3: Esau and Jacob

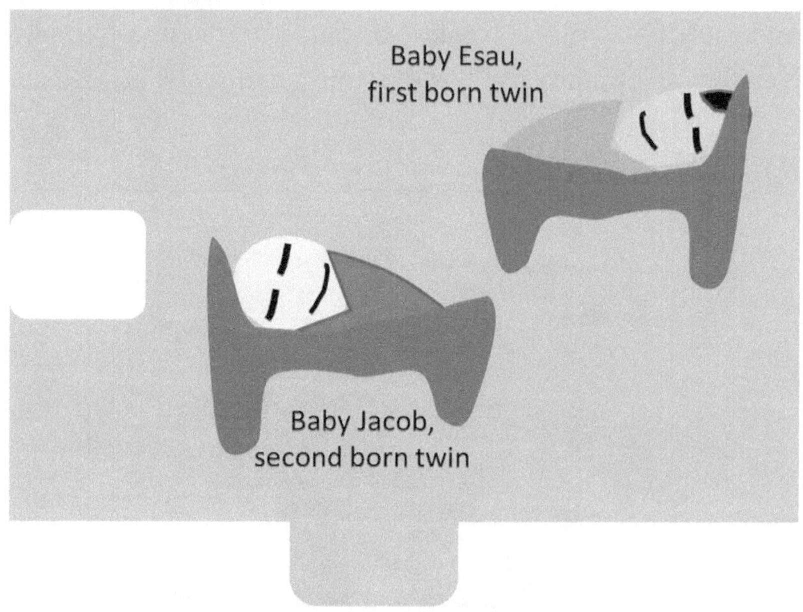

Isaac and Rebekah named their twin boys Esau and Jacob. The brothers were very different from each other. Esau enjoyed hunting and being in the wild. His skin was reddish from being out in the sun, and he was covered, from head to toe, with hair as thick as a coat. Because Isaac enjoyed the delicious, wild meat Esau always brought home, Esau was Isaac's favorite son.

Jacob was the complete opposite of Esau. Jacob was always helping out around the camp, so he was Rebekah's favorite son. He liked to stay at home, cook, and tend to the tents. His skin was light and smooth because he was around the tents all the time and out of the sun.

Because Isaac favored one son and Rebekah favored the other, their family life was full of conflict. The brothers competed with each other constantly and not in a good way. Their unhealthy family life became the foundation for generations to come.

How can competing with one another be good for us? How can it be bad for us?

Puzzle #4: Esau's first loss

An important piece of this puzzle is the Old Testament tradition of the two gifts given to a firstborn son. The birthright of his father gave the firstborn son special honor and privileges. In time, the firstborn son would become the spiritual leader and judge of the clan and receive a double portion of his father's wealth. A blessing from his father gave the firstborn son the leadership role as head of the family after the father died and went to heaven.

Well, back to the story. One day Esau was out hunting all day in the wilderness. At day's end, he stumbled back home, starved and exhausted. Jacob had spent his day cooking some of his delicious stew.

When Esau got back to the camp, he thought, "Oh, good! I am starving, but there is stew ready." Rather than asking courteously for his supper, Esau demanded a bowl of the stew.

Jacob decided to make Esau pay for his meal. Jacob said, "I will give you stew if you give me your birthright." Whoa!

Jacob and Esau both knew the power and importance of the birthright. If Esau agreed, Jacob, the younger twin, would get all the honor, privileges, power, and wealth reserved for the firstborn son. Esau put up a little bit of a fight, but Jacob wouldn't budge one bit.

Esau was so starved that he finally said, "Fine! Give me some stew! I am going to die of starvation, so what use is my birthright to me?" Esau gave up his birthright for a bowl of stew!

Esau's losses did not end with that immensely expensive bowl of stew. When Isaac was very old and could no longer see, he told his son, Esau, to go hunting and bring back his favorite game to eat. Isaac would then give Esau the blessing of the firstborn. Esau knew this blessing would guarantee his leadership role in the family after Isaac was gone. Esau immediately set out to do as his father commanded in order to get his father's blessing.

That sounds simple enough, but Rebekah overheard Isaac talking to Esau. Because Rebekah favored Jacob, she wanted Jacob, instead of Esau, to get Isaac's blessing. She quickly devised a plan to trick Isaac into giving Jacob, their second son, the blessing reserved for the firstborn son. She told Jacob to kill two young goats and cook them in the tasty way Isaac enjoyed. Then Jacob was to serve the meal to his father and get the blessing. However, Jacob saw a problem with his mother's plan.

He said, "Mother, I am smooth-skinned, not like Esau, who is hairy. And I do not smell at all like Esau. I do not think this will work because Father will certainly know I am Jacob if he touches me."

Rebekah had a plan. She told Jacob to put on some of Esau's clothes. Then she fixed the goatskin so that it covered Jacob's neck, arms, and hands. In this way, when Isaac reached out to touch Jacob, Jacob would feel and smell like Esau.

The evil trick worked. Isaac gave Jacob the blessing that was supposed to be Esau's. With that blessing, Isaac had made Jacob master over Esau and declared that all Jacob's brothers would be his servants.

Esau was distraught when he realized Jacob had tricked their father. He cried out, "Father, please give me a blessing too! Surely you have another blessing you can give me!" Isaac replied that he only had one blessing. Esau pleaded again for a blessing from his father. So Isaac gave him a blessing, as best he could. But Esau's blessing contained only hard work and pain, and it stated that Esau would still serve his younger brother, Jacob, as it is written in Genesis 27:39.

Have you ever seen someone receive something that should have been yours?

Well, when Jacob tricked Esau out of both his rightful gifts, his action led to continued rivalry and conflict between the two brothers. Esau and Jacob did not get along at all. Esau was filled with anger and hatred for Jacob. As he focused on the pain of losing his birthright and his father's blessing, his heart hardened, and he rebelled against everyone. He even started plotting to kill his brother, Jacob, after Isaac died. He rebelled in every way he could imagine. He married a woman whom his father had told him to avoid.

God was watching all this conflict. So, to help diffuse the situation, God sent Esau and his descendants to Edom and Jacob and his descendants to the promised lands of Israel and Judah. The descendants of Esau became the nation of Edom, and the descendants of Jacob became the nations of Israel and Judah. The hatred and war between the brothers passed down from generation to generation. The Edomites were always jealous of Israel and Judah. They were especially jealous that God's Temple had been built in Jerusalem, in the land of Judah.

Around 585–550 BC, God had seen enough of the hatred shown to the people of Israel and Judah by the Edomites. He sent Obadiah a vision. Obadiah saw that Yahweh (God) wanted him to deliver a message to the people of Edom. The message was the same message that both Jonah and Nahum had delivered to the Assyrians in Nineveh.

The message was that because of the Edomites' evil and wicked ways, God was going to destroy their city.

Obadiah had three points to make to the Edomites. When the Babylonians destroyed Jerusalem and God's Temple in 586 BC, the Edomites had cheered wildly. (Remember—after the floods knocked down and destroyed the hundred-foot walls of Nineveh, the Babylonians were the same warriors who had marched in and leveled the city.) After the destruction of Jerusalem, the Edomites were arrogant and prideful because their country was still standing and unharmed. They were happy that their hated relatives, the Israelites, were almost completely wiped out. God was angered by the Edomites' prideful and arrogant attitude. God was ready to punish the Edomites for their hatred and hard hearts.

What is the difference between good pride and sinful pride?

Obadiah addressed the few people who had survived all the years of war waged against them in Israel and Judah and told them: "The kingdom will be the Lord's." Obadiah reassured them that God would bring righteousness out of all the wickedness they had experienced. Obadiah also predicted that people from Negev, Philistia, Ephraim, and Samaria and exiles from Jerusalem would eventually wind up living in Edom. The people of Israel and Judah knew this message from God meant that the Edomites, their wicked, evil, unhelpful relatives, would be destroyed.

Obadiah also reassured the Israelites that Yahweh would have power over the nations. This meant many things to the people of Israel and Judah. First, the day of the Lord was coming. God's people would know it had arrived when Edom would be punished for their wicked and evil deeds. God had always decided and will always decide which nation is to be the most powerful and which rulers are to sit on the thrones and govern each nation. God promised divine justice and reminded the people of Israel and Judah that he knows about every sin.

We receive encouragement and hope from Obadiah's vision from God. God sees and hears everything. God knows our deepest secrets and thoughts. God loves us, and he is always loyal and fair. But no one who sins can avoid punishment.

If we put the puzzle pieces together, we can easily see the entire story of Obadiah's mission. What a powerful story and important lesson we can learn!

Remember the Golden Rule? As you do to others, it will be done to you. The Edomites needed a good, strong lesson in the Golden Rule. Do you agree?

What message was Obadiah to tell the people of Edom?

This story sounds like the stories of two other prophets. Who were they?

Is the book of Obadiah the shortest or longest book in the Old Testament? How long is it?

Obadiah 1:15

The day of the Lord is near for all nations. As you have done, it will be done to you; your deeds will return upon your own head.

Genesis 17:2

Then I will make my covenant between me and you and will greatly increase your numbers.

Genesis 27:39—40

His father Isaac answered him,
Your dwelling will be away from the earth's richness,
Away from the dew of heaven above. [39]

You will live by the sword and you will serve your brother. But when you grow restless, you will throw his yoke from off your neck.[40]

James 1:2—5

[2] Consider it pure joy, my brothers and sisters whenever you face trials of many kinds, [3] because you know that the testing of your faith produces perseverance. [4] Let perseverance finish its work so that you may be mature and complete, not lacking anything. [5] If any of you lacks wisdom, you should ask God, who gives generously to all without finding fault, and it will be given to you."

Prayer

Dear heavenly Father, help me remember the story of Obadiah and know that I am responsible to you for my actions. I realize that if I sin, I need to ask your forgiveness. I also know that I need to listen to you. It is good to be reminded of the Golden Rule. Please help me remember and follow it always. In your name I pray. Amen.

Puzzle

Edom
Mediterranean Sea
Dead Sea
Israel
Judah
Draw a line from each location to the place on the map.
C
A
D
E
B

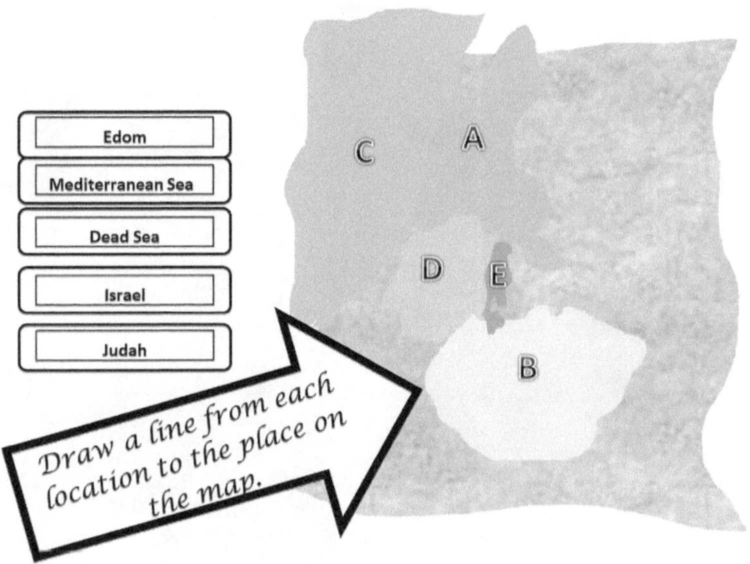

Acknowledgments

I am forever grateful to the many friends, family members, pastors, designers, and business executives who have read my books and commented. (I sometimes wonder if there is anyone who hasn't read them!) But I am especially grateful to Alexa, who is in the third grade and is one of the attendees at my church. She and her mom combed through the text and gave extremely helpful suggestions that were invaluable. It has been extremely helpful to have my book read by someone in the age bracket for which it was written.

Resources

Essentials Study Bible, New International Version NIV, Zondervan Publishing

New Inductive Study Bible, New American Standard Bible, NASB, Harvest House Publishing

Holy Bible School and Reference Edition, The John A. Hertel Co. 1955

Fast Facts Bible, New International Version NIV, 2013

Andrew W. Hill and John H. Walton, *A Survey of the Old Testament*, Second Edition, Zondervan Publishing, 2000

Holman Illustrated Bible Handbook, Holman Bible Publishing, 2012

John H. Walton, Mark L. Strauss, Ted Cooper Jr., *The Essential Bible Companion Reference*, Zondervan Publishing, 2006